# BOOK ONE

# A DOZEN A DAY SONGBOOK

## Pop Hits

**Including music from Adele, Elton John,
Coldplay, Norah Jones, Rihanna plus many more...**

Exclusive Distributors:
Music Sales Limited
Newmarket Road, Bury St Edmunds, Suffolk IP33 3YB, UK.
Music Sales Pty Limited
Units 3-4, 17 Willfox Street, Condell Park, NSW 2200, Australia.

Order No. WMR101222
ISBN: 978-1-78038-908-0

Arrangements, engravings and audio supplied by Camden Music Services.
CD audio arranged, programmed and mixed by Jeremy Birchall and Christopher Hussey.
Edited by Sam Lung.
CD recorded, mixed and mastered by Jonas Persson.

Printed in the EU.

**Your Guarantee of Quality**

As publishers, we strive to produce every book to the highest commercial standards.
This book has been carefully designed to minimise awkward page turns and to make
playing from it a real pleasure. Particular care has been given to specifying acid-free,
neutral-sized paper made from pulps which have not been elemental chlorine bleached.
This pulp is from farmed sustainable forests and was produced with special regard for
the environment. Throughout, the printing and binding have been planned to ensure a
sturdy, attractive publication which should give years of enjoyment. If your copy fails to
meet our high standards, please inform us and we will gladly replace it.

www.musicsales.com

**THE WILLIS MUSIC COMPANY**

This collection of well-known pop pieces can be used on its own or as supplementary material to the iconic *A Dozen A Day* techniques series by Edna Mae Burnam. The pieces have been arranged to progress gradually, applying concepts and patterns from Burnam's technical exercises whenever possible. Teacher accompaniments and suggested guidelines for use with the original series are also provided.

These arrangements are excellent supplements for any method and may also be used for sight-reading practice for more advanced students.

The difficulty titles of certain editions of the *A Dozen A Day* books may vary internationally. This repertoire book corresponds to the second difficulty level.

# Contents

# Make You Feel My Love

*Use with A Dozen A Day Book One, after Group I (page 9)*

**TRACKS 1–2**

Words & Music by Bob Dylan
*Arranged by Christopher Hussey*

**Expressively**

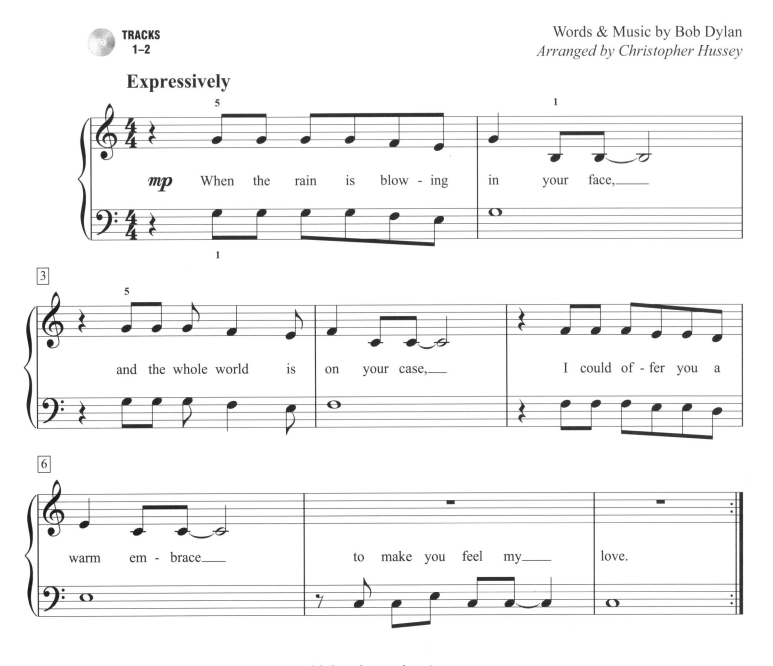

When the rain is blow-ing in your face,

and the whole world is on your case, I could of-fer you a

warm em-brace to make you feel my love.

**Accompaniment** (student plays one octave higher than written)

**Expressively**

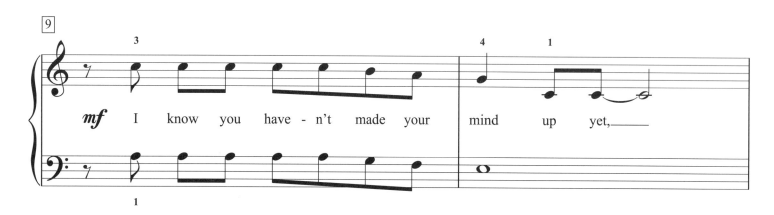

molto rit.

# Take A Bow

*Use after Group I (page 9)*

Words & Music by Mikkel Eriksen,
Tor Erik Hermansen & Shaffer Smith
*Arranged by Christopher Hussey*

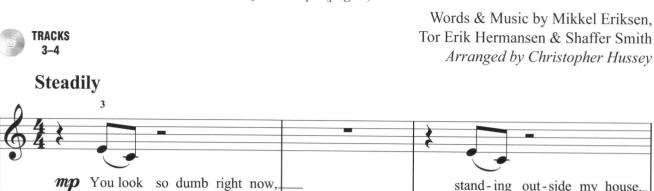

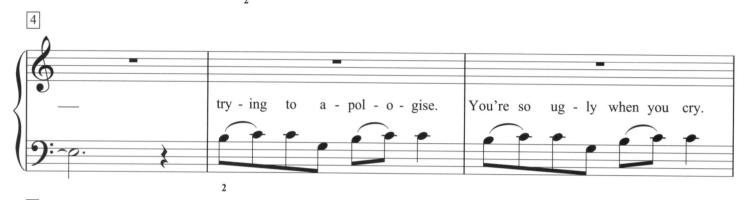

**Accompaniment** (student plays one octave higher than written)

# Eternal Flame

*Use after Group II (page 13)*

Words & Music by Susanna Hoffs,
Tom Kelly & Billy Steinberg
*Arranged by Christopher Hussey*

**TRACKS
5–6**

**Tenderly**

*mf* Close your eyes, give me your hand,___ dar - ling. Do you feel my heart

beat - ing?___ Do you un - der - stand? Do you feel the same?___ Am I on - ly

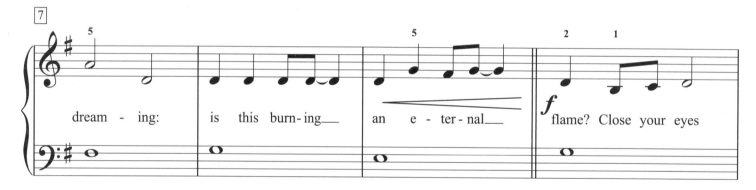

dream - ing: is this burn - ing___ an e - ter - nal___ *f* flame? Close your eyes

**Accompaniment** (student plays one octave higher than written)

**Tenderly**

## About This Activity

Ready,Set,Go! note naming speed test will challenge students to develop speed and accuracy in their note naming skills. With the clock ticking, students will name 10 notes as fast as they can. When they complete the line they record their time (incorrect answers add 5 seconds to their score). Try again. Beginner Level: 60 seconds/10 notes - Intermediate: 30 seconds/10 notes - Advanced Level: 10 seconds/10 notes.

Bass Clef (F Clef)/C Position

# Ready, Set, Go!

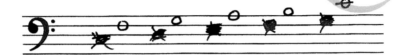

F    G    A    B    C

Min _____ Sec _____

Min _____ Sec _____

Min _____ Sec _____

Min _____ Sec _____

## About This Activity

Ready, Set, Go! note naming speed test will challenge students to develop speed and accuracy in their note naming skills. With the clock ticking, students will name 10 notes as fast as they can. When they complete the line they record their time (incorrect answers add 5 seconds to their score). Try again. Beginner Level: 60 seconds/10 notes - Intermediate: 30 seconds/10 notes - Advanced Level: 10 seconds/10 notes.

Treble Clef (G Clef)/C Position

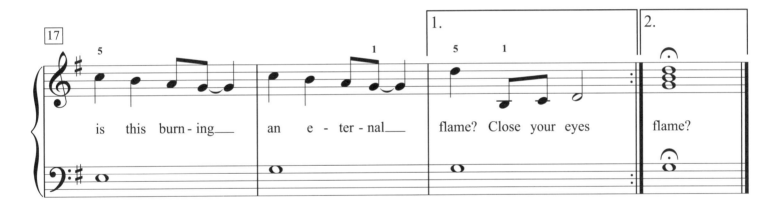

# Killing Me Softly With His Song

*Use after Group II (page 13)*

Words by Norman Gimbel
Music by Charles Fox
*Arranged by Christopher Hussey*

**TRACKS
7–8**

**Lightly, with a bounce**

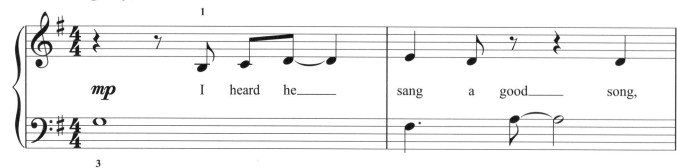

**Accompaniment** (student plays one octave higher than written)

**Lightly, with a bounce**

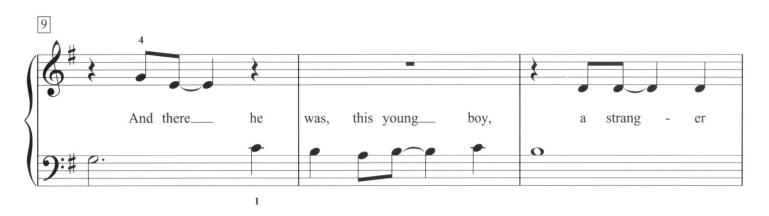

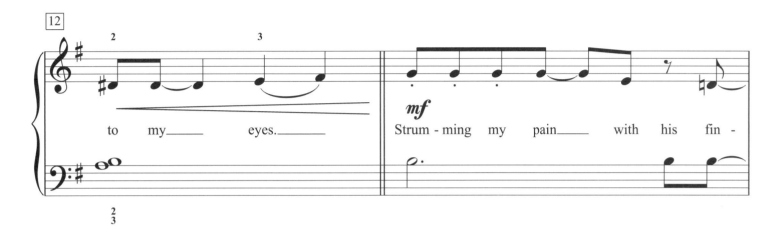

# Viva La Vida

*Use after Group III (page 18)*

Words & Music by Guy Berryman,
Jon Buckland, Will Champion & Chris Martin
*Arranged by Christopher Hussey*

**TRACKS**
**9–10**

**Energetically**

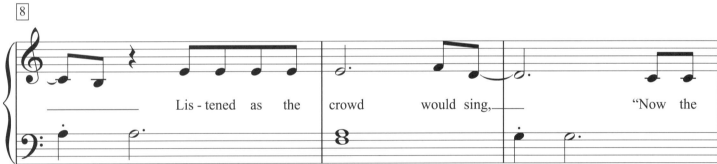

**Accompaniment** (student plays one octave higher than written)

**Energetically**

# Candle In The Wind

*Use after Group III (page 18)*

Words & Music by Elton John & Bernie Taupin
*Arranged by Christopher Hussey*

**Passionately**

Good - bye___ Nor - ma Jean, though I nev - er knew you at

all, you had___ the grace to hold your - self while those a - round___ you

crawled.___ They crawled out of the wood - work,

**Accompaniment** (student plays one octave higher than written)

**Passionately**

and they whis-pered / in - to your___ brain, they set you on a

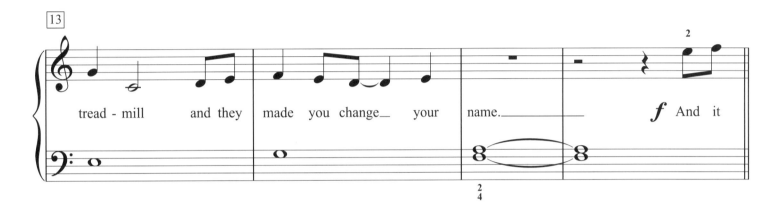

tread - mill and they / made you change___ your / name._____ / **f** And it

seems to me, you / lived your___ life like a / can - dle in___ the

wind, nev - er know - ing___ who to cling to when the

rain set in.___ And I would have___ liked to have

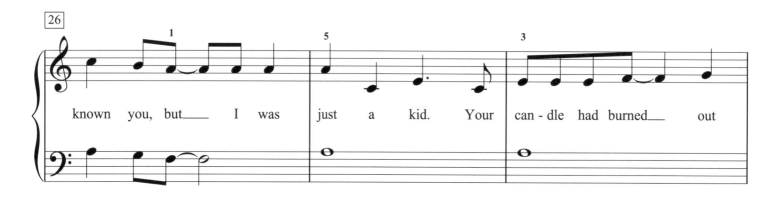

known you, but___ I was just a kid. Your can - dle had burned___ out

# Grenade

*Use after Group IV (page 24)*

Words & Music by Philip Lawrence,
Peter Hernandez, Christopher Brown,
Ari Levine, Claude Kelly & Andrew Wyatt
*Arranged by Christopher Hussey*

**TRACKS**
**13–14**

**Energetically**

Ea - sy come, ea - sy go, that's just how you live, oh.

Take, take, take it all, but you nev - er give.

Should -'ve known you was trou - ble from the first kiss, had your eyes wide o - pen. Why were they o - pen?

**Accompaniment** (student plays one octave higher than written)

**Energetically**

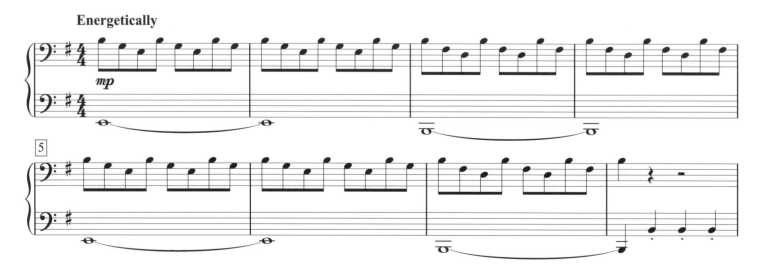

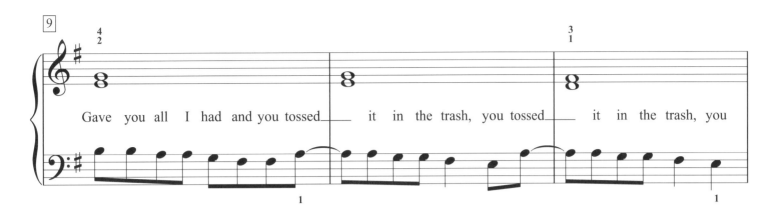

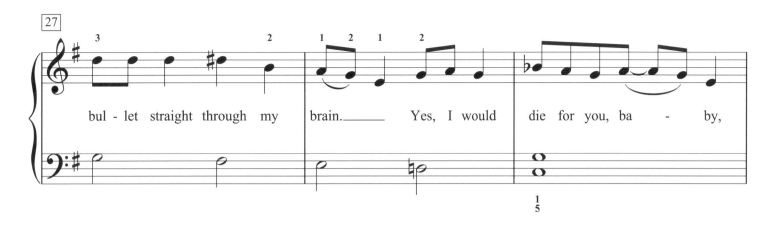

bul - let straight through my brain._____ Yes, I would die for you, ba - - by,

but you won't do the same.

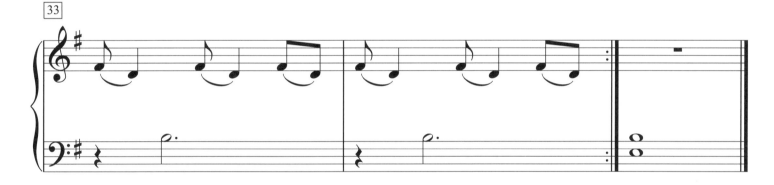

# Clocks

*Use after Group IV (page 24)*

Words & Music by Guy Berryman,
Chris Martin, Jon Buckland & Will Champion
*Arranged by Christopher Hussey*

**TRACKS 15–16**

**Accompaniment** (student plays one octave higher than written)

brought me down up - on my___ knees. Oh, I beg, I beg and___ plead, sing - ing...

Come out with things un - said, shoot an ap - ple off my___ head, and a

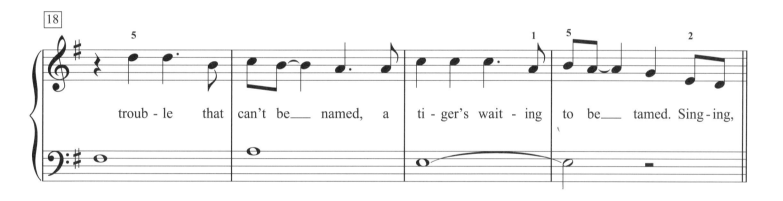

troub - le that can't be___ named, a ti - ger's wait - ing to be___ tamed. Sing - ing,

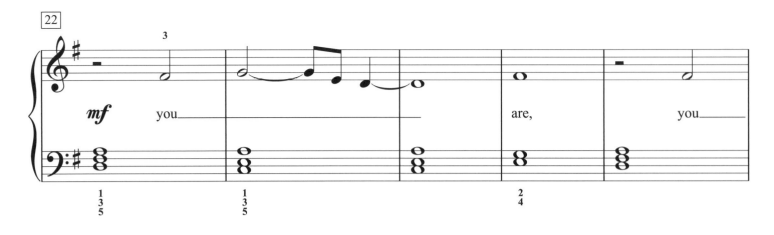

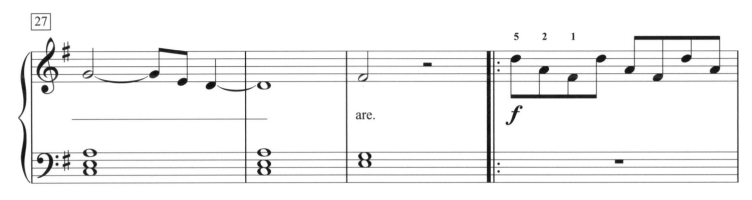

# Don't Know Why

*Use after Group V (page 31)*

**TRACKS 17–18**

Words & Music by Jesse Harris
*Arranged by Christopher Hussey*

**Relaxedly**

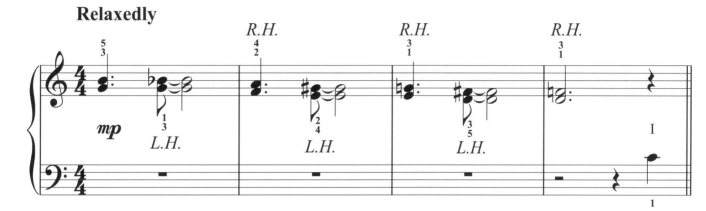

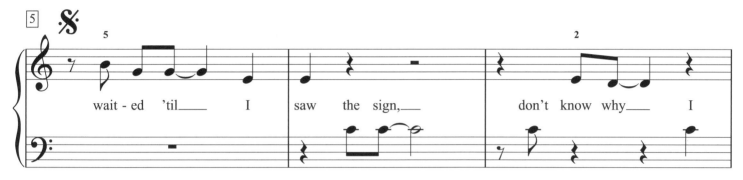

wait - ed 'til___ I saw the sign,___ don't know why___ I

did - n't come. I left you by___ the house of fun,___

**Accompaniment** (student plays one octave higher than written)

**Relaxedly**

don't know why___ I did - n't come, I don't know why___ I

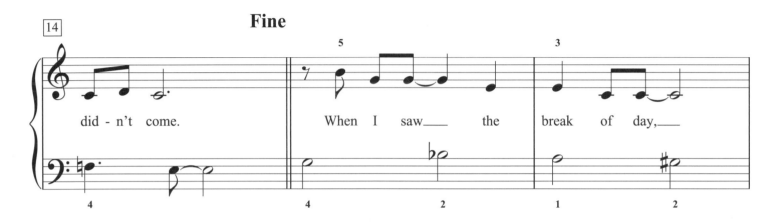

**Fine**

did - n't come. When I saw___ the break of day,___

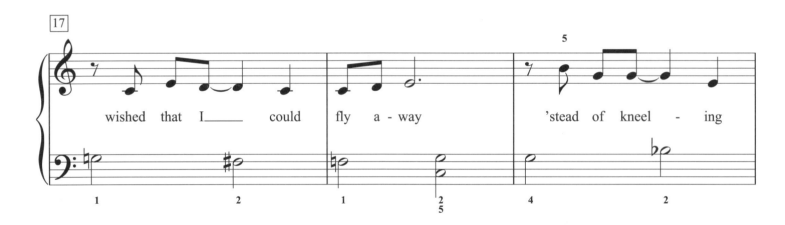

wished that I___ could fly a - way 'stead of kneel - ing

**Fine**

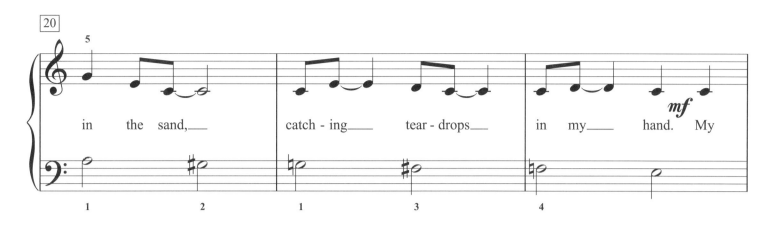

D.S. al Fine

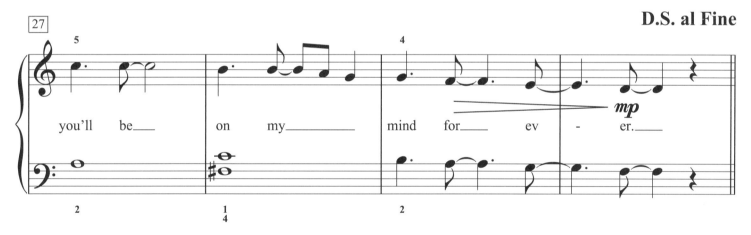

D.S. al Fine

# Close To You (They Long To Be)

*Use after Group V (page 31)*

Words by Hal David
Music by Burt Bacharach
*Arranged by Christopher Hussey*

TRACKS
19–20

**Accompaniment** (student plays one octave higher than written)